Original title:
Rhymes with Relativity

Copyright © 2025 Creative Arts Management OÜ
All rights reserved.

Author: Sophia Kingsley
ISBN HARDBACK: 978-1-80567-859-5
ISBN PAPERBACK: 978-1-80567-980-6

The Metrics of Mystery

In a world where clocks twist and twirl,
Even seconds seem to dance and swirl.
A cat on a skateboard whizzes by,
Waving at squirrels in the sky.

Time ticks like a chicken's beat,
Wobbling on tiny, clumsy feet.
Gravity pulls with a playful hug,
While planets share a cosmic shrug.

The math is scribbled all askew,
Chalkboard notes in shades of blue.
Einstein's hair is now a hat,
As I ponder where my lunch went flat.

In this circus of cosmic cheer,
Laughter echoes, loud and near.
We spin through life, a merry chase,
In the metrics of this goofy space.

Gravity's Lullaby in the Void

In the dark where space is wide,
Things float freely, none can hide.
A cat in dreams begins to purr,
While planets waltz, and comets stir.

A star tickles a black hole's cheek,
With every giggle, they both sneak.
Round and round in endless loops,
As cosmic owls hoot in goofy groups.

Temporal Tides and Stellar Rides

Time tickles as we surf the waves,
Bouncing off clocks and cosmic caves.
The future's late; the past won't budge,
And present moments subtly trudge.

A wormhole's twist, a sideway slide,
Where time's a joke, and we all glide.
Make sure to laugh along the way,
Or risk getting lost in yesterday.

Harmonies of the Quantum Sea

In a sea of quarks, we twist and dive,
Where particles dance and barely jive.
Wave-particle, who are you?
A funny game of peekaboo.

Entangled socks and tangled hair,
As Schrödinger smiles from his cozy chair.
With a wink and a grin, he shakes his head,
At all the theories that people spread.

The Art of Being: A Cosmic Tale

Once upon a time, or maybe twice,
The universe spun with sugar and spice.
With aliens that joke; they sip tea,
And ponder the wonders of all we see.

A cosmic artist paints with stars,
Giving birth to planets and funny Mars.
In this grand tale where giggles thrive,
The art of being is to just survive.

Harmonies of the Heavens

A comet sneezed, a planet laughed,
The moon made jokes, a cosmic craft.
Stars waltzed wildly, in a dance so bright,
While meteors cracked puns in the night.

Galaxies giggled, swirling in glee,
Black holes told stories, oh couldn't we see!
Asteroids chuckled, rolling on by,
In this universe, humor surely won't die.

The Measure of Moments

Time ticked funny, with a twist and a bend,
Every second laughed, it just wouldn't end.
Clock hands wobbled, like jelly on toast,
Counting the giggles, that's what we boast.

With each heartbeat, chuckles we find,
Moments of joy, joyfully aligned.
Sundials grinned, shadows took flight,
In the measure of moments, we're feelin' just right.

Stars in Suspense

Twinkling stars plotted a heist,
To steal the night, and that felt nice.
Jupiter juggled, while Venus took bets,
And Saturn just laughed at the whole silly sets.

Each nova a joke, bright bursts on display,
Galactic reveals, come join in the play!
Stars held their breath, then burst out in cheer,
In the grand cosmic circus, it's all quite clear.

Tidal Waves of Time

Waves of space broke on the shore,
Surfboards of light flew evermore.
Time surfed on curls of an ocean so vast,
Riding the tides, it giggled, it laughed.

Each splash a memory, flickers of fun,
Ebbing and flowing, never to shun.
On this beach of existence, we play and we chime,
Laughing and splashing in tidal waves of time.

Celestial Chorus

Stars twinkle in a sly ballet,
Winking down in a cosmic play.
Galaxies swirl with a cheeky grin,
As black holes chuckle, 'Let the fun begin!'

Comets race in a dizzy spree,
Faceplant in orbits, oh what glee!
Nebulas dance, all colors abound,
While aliens giggle, their laughter resounds.

Luminary Lullabies

Moonbeams croon a sleepy tune,
To planets who sway beneath the moon.
Saturn spins in a jazzy sweep,
While Jupiter sighs, drifting to sleep.

Shooting stars trade winks and laughs,
They tumble and roll like quirky drafts.
Dancing shadows on Martian plains,
Sing lullabies to ease cosmic pains.

The Space in Between

In the void, a giggle grows,
Whispers of stars, no one knows.
Asteroids wiggle, oh so spry,
As meteors zoom with a goofy sigh.

Wormholes play hide and seek,
Twisting reality, oh so unique.
Time does somersaults in delight,
While physics takes a break tonight.

Planetary Palindromes

Planets spin, round and round,
Making jokes that are quite sound.
"Is it a star, or just my hat?"
Said Mars to Venus, how 'bout that!

They swap tales of their strange days,
In circles of laughter, merry plays.
Cosmic riddles are all the hype,
With a punchline at the end of the type.

The Alignment of Aspects

When planets dance in crazy spins,
They juggle moons like playful twins.
Gravity's a comical treat,
As stardust tickles our two left feet.

In cosmos parties, stars collide,
They laugh and whirl, with comets wide.
Black holes gulp like hungry beasts,
While aliens share galactic feasts.

The sun winks at the cosmic show,
While meteors zoom in a silly flow.
Orbiting clowns in a solar game,
Chasing photons, they're never the same.

So here's to space, a whimsical ride,
With side-splitting jokes from the universe wide.
Join in the laughter, don't miss the fun,
In the maze of cosmos, we're all one by one.

Frequencies of Forever

Tune in to the cosmic frequency,
Where laughter echoes with glee.
Wave your hands, it's quite the sight,
Dancing to tunes from day to night.

A quasar hums a silly song,
While neutron stars join in along.
Their musical notes twist and twirl,
In this odd space, we all unfurl.

Alien DJs spin the decks,
Mixing time like crazy wrecks.
Beats from light years come crashing near,
Every note brings another cheer.

Join the band in the astral spree,
Where nonsense reigns in harmony.
In the vastness, we laugh together,
Creating joy that lasts forever.

Celestial Cartography

Scout the heavens with a map so bright,
Drawn by starlight on a magical night.
Comets leave trails like paint on a way,
While space penguins dance with much to say.

Planets gossip, they share their dreams,
About adventures in starry streams.
Saturn spins rings in the ultimate style,
Winking at Earth with a cheeky smile.

Zigzagging through the Milky Way maze,
While curious meteors set hearts ablaze.
"Where's the nearest black hole?" one asks wide-eyed,
"To take us home on a cosmic ride!"

In this swirling map of fun and glee,
We chart the cosmos with wild esprit.
So pack your compass, don't hesitate,
For joy in the stars is a funny fate.

Space-time Serenades

A serenade of the stars begins,
As cosmic giggles swirl with spins.
Time twists in a comical knot,
As spacetime dances and laughs a lot.

Planets croon their melodic notes,
Shooting stars ride on whimsical boats.
Neutron dancers lead with flair,
While stardust tickles in the airy chair.

In the symphony of the night so grand,
Even black holes can't resist to stand.
They sway and twirl, what a delight,
Singing praises to the vast starlight.

So lift your voice to the heavens high,
Join the chorus, let laughter fly.
In this orchestra of space and time,
The serendipity of joy is in every rhyme.

The Language of Stars and Echoes

In the night, the stars do prance,
Giggling as they take a chance.
They whisper tales of cosmic glee,
Making jokes we cannot see.

Planets waltz in silly hats,
Comets ride on friendly bats.
Each twinkle's just a big surprise,
Like shooting stars with goofy eyes.

The moons they laugh in craters wide,
Bouncing off the galactic tide.
Constellations play charades,
As meteors throw grand parades.

So let's dance beneath this show,
Where echoes giggle, ebb, and flow.
With every glance at skies so bright,
We'll find the humor in the night.

Beyond Horizons: The Weight of Now

Floating high above the rest,
Time decides to take a jest.
Hours tiptoe on a tightrope,
As seconds spin with all their hope.

The past is just a funny ghost,
It haunts the present, makes the most.
Now is like a balloon gone pop,
Bouncing wildly, can't be stopped.

Horizons stretch like silly strings,
While time itself just laughs and sings.
Each moment's shaped like silly putty,
Where worries feel a bit too nutty.

So grab a second, hold it tight,
And enjoy the quirky flight.
When things get heavy, look above,
And find the weight is made of love.

Whispers of Eternity in the Night

The night-time's full of chuckling dreams,
With moonbeams dancing, or so it seems.
Stars giggle softly, jokes unsaid,
As stories weave through sleepy head.

Eternity whispers in a playful tone,
Tickling the mind when you're alone.
In shadows deep, the laughter grows,
Crafting tales where silliness flows.

A cosmic jest, a timeless game,
Each whispered secret, never the same.
Tick-tock, the clock joins in the fun,
As night embraces the morning sun.

So in the dark, let laughter rise,
With every sparkle, spin bright ties.
For in this night, the world seems right,
Whispers sing, 'Hold on tight!'

Cosmic Threads Weaving Fate

Threads of fate all twist and twirl,
Each one dances, gives a whirl.
The universe is quite the seamstress,
Stitching laughs, oh what a mess!

Galaxies play a game of tag,
While supernovas burst and brag.
Cosmic yarns, in colors bright,
Weave the stories of delight.

Planets chuckle, spinning round,
As tiny meteors fall on ground.
Each thread pulled tighter brings a grin,
For fun's the secret held within.

So let's embrace this cosmic fate,
Where every twist brings laughs so great.
In this fabric of the night,
Laughter's woven, pure delight.

A Symphony of Celestial Waves

Stars twinkle and wink, a cosmic show,
Planets groove in their orbits, oh so slow.
Space cats strum guitars on the rings of Mars,
While comets juggle sparkles, beneath the stars.

Asteroids dance with flair, a wobbly spree,
Galaxies swirl like ice cream, just wait and see.
With every cosmic note, a laugh we find,
In the symphony of space, we're all intertwined.

Quantum giggles echo through the black,
As photons play tag on a light-speed track.
With cosmic tickles and playful pranks,
The universe chuckles at our silly ranks.

So join the fun, step into the night,
Where the cosmos hums with sheer delight.
In this vast opera, we all have a part,
As waves of laughter ripple through the heart.

Dancing Shadows on the Cosmic Canvas

Sketching dreams with starlight, shadows play,
On the cosmic easel, they twirl and sway.
Planets paint the night with a vibrant hue,
While moonbeams slap paint on the canvas, too.

Brushes made of meteors, flick and swirl,
Creating cosmic patterns, a galactic whirl.
Each stroke a giggle, each splash a cheer,
In the art of the universe, let's persevere.

Nebulas puff colors with a playful flair,
As comets race by without a single care.
Dancing shadows join the stellar parade,
In the gallery of space, no moment's delayed.

So grab your palette, and join the spree,
As stardust whispers, "Come dance with me!"
With laughter and joy, paint the night bright,
In the tapestry of space, we shine just right.

Enigma of Moments in a Cosmic Spree

Tick-tock goes the clock in a timeless feat,
Moments bounce by like a cosmic retreat.
Each second's a prankster, mischief untold,
As time dips and spins, like marbles of gold.

Wormholes are shortcuts for moments to play,
Jumping through loops like kids at the bay.
Laughter echoes through space in a swirl,
As we twirl in the dance of a celestial whirl.

Chronicles flutter like leaves in the breeze,
Telling tales of the universe, aiming to please.
With every giggle caught in a star,
We float in the mystique of who we are.

So let's chase those seconds, don't let them go,
Join the cosmic spree, and let laughter flow.
For in this enigma, we're all part of the fun,
Unraveling mysteries till the day is done.

Lightyears Apart, Yet So Close

Across the vast expanse, we wave and shout,
Lightyears may part us, but we're never left out.
In the cosmic café, we sip on our dreams,
Sharing stories of laughter, or so it seems.

Galactic phone calls are quite the delight,
With a delay in giggles, but that's all right.
We're sharing our secrets through pulses of light,
Joking about how we're both out of sight.

Even when distances stretch like a face,
Friendship binds us in this infinite race.
Like photons in sync, we shimmer and glow,
In the depths of the cosmos, we always know.

So let's laugh at the distance, it's all good fun,
For in this universe, we're never outdone.
Through the cosmic web, our joy knows no bounds,
Lightyears may separate, but laughter resounds.

The Compass of Chaos

In a place where ducks wear hats,
And squirrels engage in acrobats,
A compass spins in pure dismay,
Guiding us the wacky way.

In a world where clocks run slow,
Every hour is much too dough,
Tick-tock laughs as time goes wild,
Like a mischievous, playful child.

The map is drawn in crayon hues,
Leading to the land of blues,
Where jellybeans grow on trees,
Dancing in the gentle breeze.

Oh, let us roam this crazy land,
With giggles, frolics, hand in hand,
For in this topsy-turvy dream,
Life's a funny, swirling scheme.

Stellar Stories

In the sky where stars confess,
Planets play a lovely game of chess,
With rockets zooming on a spree,
And aliens sipping herbal tea.

Comets dash like caffeinated mice,
While moons create a disco slice,
Asteroids wear top hats and bow,
Making sure to take a bow.

Galaxies tweet with cosmic flair,
Sharing gossip from who knows where,
With a wink, they dance and twirl,
In this delightful, starry whirl.

Oh, tell me tales of space's glee,
Of shooting stars and cups of tea,
For here, the universe feels bright,
Wrapped in laughter and pure light.

Constellation Chronicles

In the night where shapes align,
Triangles shout, "Hey, I'm divine!"
While bears and bulls engage in fights,
Making shapes on starry nights.

The Big Dipper spills some tea,
For the Little Bear to see,
Together they giggle and chase,
In the cosmic circus space.

Those shimmering dots have tales to spin,
Of fluffs and puffs where dreams begin,
With every twinkle and every wink,
They plot a giggle with a wink.

Oh, come and hear the starry lore,
Where every sleep has tales in store,
In the chronicles of the night,
Laughter sparkles, pure delight.

Waves of Wonder

Down by the shore, the waves giggle,
Chasing crabs that dance and wiggle,
Seashells whisper in the sand,
As seaweed makes a merry band.

In puddles, fish wear tiny shoes,
As dolphins share the latest news,
While jellyfish float with grace,
In this whimsical, watery place.

The sun creates a sky-high slide,
For surfers on a joy-filled ride,
Splashing colors, laughter flows,
As the ocean dances, and joy grows.

Oh, let the waves sing their sweet song,
As we dance along where we belong,
For every splash holds endless fun,
In our world of laughter and sun.

Eternal Dance of Celestial Chance

Stars in the sky do twirl and spin,
Cosmic chuckles and playful grins.
Planets jiggle in a wobbly show,
While comets flinch in a dazzling flow.

Galaxies giggle, they know the tune,
Shooting stars wiggle under the moon.
Nebulas puff out cotton candy fluff,
In this vast space, life's silly and tough.

Meteors bounce like they're in a race,
Jupiter's storms have a frothy face.
Saturn's rings jingle, they dance with glee,
In this wild universe, they bumble with me.

So here we unwind with laughter in flight,
As rockets balloon and drift out of sight.
The cosmos chuckles, a raucous blast,
In this eternal dance, let joy be vast.

Quantum Dreams in Cosmic Streams

Atoms caper in a jig of surprise,
Wiggling whimsically under the skies.
Quarks and leptons spin round in delight,
In a universe giggling, from day into night.

Photons frolic in a playful maze,
Zipping through starlight in dizzying ways.
Gravity tickles the fabric of dreams,
As Schrödinger chuckles at fanciful schemes.

In this bizarre net of twinkling chance,
Every particle joins in a quirky dance.
Waves of laughter ripple through the air,
As electrons giggle in their lively affair.

So let's ride the beams of this playful flow,
In quantum wonders, let merriment grow.
With each tiny leap, a silliness gleams,
In cosmic currents, we weave our dreams.

The Measure of Space Between Hearts

Distances shrink under laughter's glow,
Hearts that twinkle like stars in a show.
In this vast void where friendships rise,
    Giggles become our sweetest ties.

Coordinates blur, the laughter's a map,
With tickles and whispers, we share a tap.
From galaxies far to the close and the near,
In each knowing glance, we banish the fear.

Moments connect like threads made of light,
Winking and grinning, we dance through the night.
In the geometry of joy, we've found a way,
To make each heartbeat a reason to play.

So come take a trip through this heart's embrace,
A journey of chuckles, a joyous chase.
In the measure of love, let's laugh and unite,
For in every space, there's always delight.

Time's Whisper and Gravity's Pull

Tick-tock's a jester, a mischievous sprite,
Pulling us close, then slipping from sight.
Slips through our fingers like sand on the shore,
Time giggles gently, then winks and will soar.

Gravity chuckles, it hugs us too tight,
Like a parent who laughs while scaring the light.
Dancing in circles, we swirl in the breeze,
As moments respond to our quirks with ease.

Seconds can tickle; they can also delay,
Laughter's the currency, come join in the play.
Time gives a nod, while we spin, twist, and whirl,
In this cosmic comedy, laughter's our pearl.

So let's jest with the hours and frolic with days,
In this wondrous spectacle, let's giggle and sway.
For in this grand scheme, what truly can rule,
Is Time's whispering magic and Gravity's pull.

The Rhythms of Reality

In the dance of the stars, we twirl with glee,
Gravity's pull can't keep us from spree.
Time ticks away, like a jester's laugh,
Do the worm for a lightyear, feel the cosmic half.

Space is a party, the comets spin,
Black holes are circles, where fun begins.
With aliens laughing, we can't help but cheer,
Just watch out for wars over popcorn and beer.

Nebulas swirl like a painter's delight,
While shooting stars wink, they say, "What a night!"
We'll juggle the planets, harmonize the moons,
Losing track of the time, 'cause it's always cartoons!

So let's play some hopscotch on Saturn's rings,
And giggle through galaxies, oh what joy! It brings!
Reality's rhythm, a comedy show,
With laughter resounding, forever we'll flow.

Cosmic Reflections

In mirrors of space, what a sight to behold,
Galaxies giggle, their stories retold.
Planets play peek-a-boo, round and round,
While stardust confetti rains down from the sound.

Quasars act silly, lighting the path,
While black holes make jokes about cosmic math.
Time-traveling turtles with hats on their heads,
Sing songs to the comets, like playful threads.

Invisible friends twirl with ethereal flair,
In the vast universe, there's fun everywhere.
With photons that tickle, and electrons that tease,
We'll ride on light beams, sailing space with ease!

So grab a space rocket, let's lift off and see,
This wild cosmic circus is where we're meant to be.
With laughter in stardust, we'll dance through the night,
Cosmic reflections, a glorious sight!

Echoes from Eons

From ages of yore, the echoes resound,
Time-hopping jesters leap up from the ground.
With giggles from giants and whispers from stars,
The cosmos is chuckling, it's written in scars.

Eons are all just a big, silly game,
With time-lords and gnomes, who knows who's to blame?

Clouds of old laughter, swirling in space,
The universe chuckles, keeping a pace.

Dinosaurs danced with asteroids bright,
As meteors zipped with delight through the night.
Fossils now tell tales of a time full of fun,
Where the roars of the past echo, a galactic pun.

So join in the tapestries, weave a fine thread,
With echoes of laughter, we'll dance instead.
For in every eon, there's joy to uplift,
With humor so cosmic, it's the ultimate gift!

Astral Artistry

The cosmos a canvas, with colors so bright,
Stars dip in paint, creating pure light.
With brushstrokes of comets, and swirls of the moon,
The universe croons its whimsical tune.

Asteroids pose like models in style,
While supernovas sparkle and twirl for a while.
And meteors play hopscotch on cosmic winds,
As laughter and joy are where the fun begins.

Galactic graffiti on the Milky Way wall,
With planets all frolicking, heed the call!
In this astral gallery, art's an escape,
While quarks bring a chuckle to this playful landscape.

So paint me a star, drop a comet in zest,
With the colors of laughter, we'll craft the best fest.
For in this vast universe, a masterpiece grows,
A funny, bright show, where joy freely flows.

Dances of the Dimensions

In a world where time gets quite loose,
A cat in a hat lets out a big moose.
They twirl through the stars, it's quite a sight,
Chasing cosmic tacos in the pale moonlight.

The clocks are all dizzy, they spin and they sway,
As jellybeans bounce in a bright, silly way.
The wormholes giggle as they twist and they bend,
Who knew space could throw such a giggly blend?

A fish rides a comet, oh what a parade,
With shoes made of jelly, a delicate spade.
They leap over black holes, yodeling cheer,
In this dance of delight, there's nothing to fear.

So grab your old fidget and shake it about,
Let's revel in chaos and have a good shout.
For in this funny universe we all exist,
The rhythm of nonsense is hard to resist.

Echoes of Enigma

In a realm where whispers trade secrets well,
A sock puppet's waltz makes the cosmos swell.
They giggle and prance as the planets align,
Turning ordinary times into forms quite divine.

Quasars chuckle as they blink in the dark,
While shadows engage in a quizzical lark.
A sandwich sits pondering under a tree,
"Is time just a joke? Could it really be me?"

Glimmers of laughter echo through space,
As comets break out in a wild, silly race.
With candy floss stardust sprinkling the night,
Every twinkling star has a mischievous bite.

An octopus juggles the moons with a grin,
While a rubber duck sings a galactic hymn.
In this peculiar dance of our universe wide,
The echoes of enigma are hard to abide.

The Universe's Underbelly

In the belly of space, where the odd likes to roam,
A spaceship made out of cheese finds a home.
With pickles as planets and ketchup as seas,
They glide through the galaxies, floating with ease.

Dancing in circles, a toaster and cat,
Who knew they'd collide in a whimsical spat?
With interstellar pancakes served atop a sun,
The brunch of the cosmos is laughably fun.

As strings of spaghetti twirl past a star,
They hum catchy tunes, driving jellybeans far.
Beneath this odd surface, the giggles abound,
In the universe's underbelly, joy can be found.

So laugh with the meteors, burst out in glee,
For space is a playground, wild and carefree.
Each crevice and corner harbors a jest,
In a quirky expanse that's simply the best.

Stellar Verses

In the realm of stars where the laughter ignites,
A pogo stick comet takes off through the nights.
With verses that shimmer like glitter on cake,
They bounce off the planets, a whimsical flake.

The orbits are filled with a carnival flair,
Where broccoli astronauts float in mid-air.
With giggling dimensions that tickle the fates,
They're writing their stories on cosmic plates.

As aliens dance with umbrellas of light,
They giggle and whirl, creating pure delight.
Each quirk in the cosmos sings back with a cheer,
In these stellar verses, the fun's ever near.

So join in the rhythms where gravity bends,
In this spectacular space where nonsense transcends.
With each twinkling poem, the universe plays,
In the laughter of stars, we rejoice and we blaze.

The Fabric of Dreams and Starlight

In a world where socks can fly,
And jellybeans can touch the sky.
The stars wear hats adorned with lights,
While giggling comets race through nights.

A moonbeam tickles a sleeping tree,
As crickets sing a symphony.
Pancakes dance beneath the sun,
And time stands still just for fun.

Quirky clouds with silly grins,
Play leapfrog over hills and bins.
Where rainbows slide down candy streams,
And nothing's ever as it seems.

So let's embrace this playful scheme,
For life's just one grand, wacky dream.
With giggles echoing through the night,
We'll stride together, hearts alight.

Celestial Coordinates of the Soul

In the attic of the Milky Way,
Martians play hopscotch every day.
With cosmic jump ropes made of stars,
They leap past dancing candy cars.

A space cat serenades the moon,
While asteroids hum a fuzzy tune.
Galaxies twirl in a wacky race,
And laughter fills the timeless space.

Cosmic dust collects in jars,
As planets search for friendly cars.
A comet slips on cosmic slime,
And giggles bounce through endless time.

Shooting stars are keen to share,
Their popcorn secrets in the air.
In every twinkle, joy awaits,
With space-folk dancing on celestial plates.

Timeless Footprints on a Celestial Shore

On shores where stardust meets the breeze,
Footprints bubble, giggle, and tease.
Sandcastles built with moonbeam light,
As fairies host a starry night.

Tidal waves of laughter crash,
As shooting stars make a splash.
The ocean sings in bubble notes,
While jellyfish wear tiny coats.

Seashells hum tales of silly fish,
Who grant your quirkiest heart's wish.
With sand between your toes of gold,
The universe's secrets unfold.

So dance upon this cosmic shore,
With heart and soul, let's laugh some more.
For on this path of playful dreams,
We'll chase the stars, or so it seems.

Orbiting the Heart of What Will Be

Around the sun, a duck does glide,
With cosmic buddies by its side.
They quack in perfect harmony,
In a solar dance of jubilee.

With rubber donuts floating high,
And sparkling sprinkles on the sky.
They race on marshmallow comets bright,
In a silly, star-studded flight.

Galactic games keep spirits light,
As meteors burst in colors bright.
Each tumble through the cosmic maze,
Unleashes laughter, sparks, and rays.

So let us orbit joyfully,
In orbits made of glee and glee!
For in this vast and playful spree,
We'll find the heart of what will be.

Celestial Vignettes of Time and Space

In a cosmic dance, we spin and twirl,
Stars wink at us, giving fate a whirl.
Floating tea cups on Jupiter's ride,
Where gravity's rules are tossed aside.

Martians wear hats, all shiny and bright,
Having a picnic on a Sunday night.
With sandwiches flying, they giggle and play,
While Saturn's rings serve cake on a tray.

Asteroids bump with a humorous thump,
In this galaxy where we leap and jump.
Nebulae laugh, like a fluffy cloud,
In their infinite joy, they sing out loud.

Kaleidoscope visions from afar collide,
Painting the void where quirks abide.
In space, we're silly, wrapped in delight,
Dancing with planets beneath starlit light.

Shadows of Infinity in the Heart

In shadows we find a playful tease,
Whispers of laughter on a cosmic breeze.
Countless echoes of love's wild flight,
Chasing the stardust deep into the night.

Fleeting moments like sparkly dust,
In this heart of darkness, we place our trust.
Tickling the void, we jump and sway,
Every heartbeat is a ballet on display.

Giggles bounce from galaxies near,
Jokes of the cosmos, oh so sincere.
A serenade of silly space sounds,
Where mirth and joy in the void resound.

Even the black holes can't hide their cheer,
As stars throw confetti, year after year.
With hearts intertwined, we embrace the scheme,
In this funny dance of a cosmic dream.

Gravity's Gentle Pull on Everyday Lives.

Everyday antics under a sunbeam,
We wobble and drift, life's comedic theme.
With gravity's tug, we trip and we fall,
Making a spectacle, we laugh through it all.

Puddles await to splash, oh what fun,
In this grand circus, we dash and run.
Each silly moment, a buoyant delight,
Life's ups and downs in endless flight.

Walking on tightropes between dreams and schemes,
Falling right into the silliest themes.
As planets spin in their dance with time,
We craft our own rhythm, raucous and prime.

So grab a balloon, let the laughter rise,
In this cosmic show, we wear our surprise.
With gravity's grip, we hover and play,
In this zany existence, come laugh and sway!

Celestial Connections.

In the universe vast, we make funny links,
Stars scribble notes while the Milky Way winks.
Grinning comets across the night sky,
Sharing teas over moon pies as they fly.

Celestial buddies, all dressed up in hues,
Passing around the latest space news.
A supernova party where we all ignite,
Dance on the moons, oh what a sight!

Through cosmic whispers and giggles we share,
A friendship so vast, beyond any compare.
Counting the meteors, we share a laugh,
As stardust brings joy on our cosmic path.

Bouncing around like electrons in glee,
Under the heavens, just you and me.
In this whimsical realm of planets and beams,
We weave our own tales, as bright as our dreams.

Twilight Tales

The moon wore a hat, quite silly and pink,
While stars played hopscotch down by the sink.
They giggled and wiggled, a cosmic charade,
Building a rocket from lemonade.

A cat with a tie danced shuffle and shake,
While shadows discussed how much time they could take.

A clock with a beard said, 'I'm never on time!'
As laughter erupted, quite loud and sublime.

Galactic Gatherings

In a nebula park, the aliens meet,
With popcorn made from interstellar wheat.
They share silly jokes that float on the breeze,
While comets attempt to do pirouettes with ease.

There's a rocket-shaped taco that's stealing the show,
Driving asteroids wild with its spicy old flow.
A dance party starts with a wormhole DJ,
Who plays all the hits from the Milky Way.

Aetherial Arpeggios

On the strings of existence, a plucker named Clyde,
Strummed tunes that made gravity swirl and glide.
The planets all jazzy, they bopped to the beat,
Though one stuck in orbit tripped over his feet.

With a wink and a nod, the sun hummed along,
While comets with saxophones played with such strong.
Twirling through measures of cosmic delight,
They danced through the darkness, from morning to night.

Timelines and Teardrops

A time traveler tripped on his own tangled past,
While laughs echoed out, they were meant to last.
He slipped on a teardrop from a star's laughing eye,
And landed in socks made of clouds in the sky.

The future was bright, with a tinge of weird,
As robots wore hats and the kittens all cheered.
In the mix, a rainbow did cartwheels and flips,
While giggles painted time with solar eclipse.

Illusions of Infinity

In a world that goes round, oh so absurd,
Where cats chase their tails, it's truly unheard.
Time bends like a straw, so bendy and bright,
We laugh at the clocks, they've lost all their might.

The numbers run wild, like a herd of lost sheep,
They dance on the page, while we try not to weep.
Cosmic confetti falls from the sky,
We're all stuck in loops, oh me, oh my!

Mirrors reflect what we wish to see,
But feedback's a joke, it's not really me.
Thoughts twirl in circles, like ice cream on cones,
We giggle at reason, it's all made of stones.

So let's toast to the quirks of reality's game,
With each twist and turn, it's never the same.
In the space where we frolic, let laughter abide,
For in silly illusions, we take cosmic pride.

Gravity's Dance

Oh gravity's pulling, don't take it too hard,
We all love a fall, though it leaves us jarred.
The ground gives a hug, a firm, hearty clutch,
But I trip on my shoelace—it loves me too much!

Planets do twirls in their cosmic ballet,
While I just wobble in the strangest of ways.
The moon winks at me, like a cheeky old friend,
As I stumble around, trying not to offend.

Jump high for a moment, feel light as a feather,
Then crash to the ground—ain't it all light as a tether?
So let's cha-cha through space, and boogie with stars,
In this dance of delight, we're all from afar.

With laughter in orbit, let's spin round and round,
For in the great universe, joy can be found.
Gravity's got rhythm, a curious chance,
As we twirl through the void in a cosmic dance.

The Rhythm of Relevance

Tick-tock goes the clock, why is it so sly?
Time's got a riddle, just like a pie.
Each slice is a moment, absurd and quite neat,
But confusion erupts when I can't find my seat.

Notes of eccentricity serenade the air,
As relevance wanders like a cat unaware.
A rhyme and a reason, they giggle and swing,
But lose their fine steps at the silliest thing.

We ponder in circles, yet never conclude,
While answers do cartwheels, they're rather rude.
So let's clap to the chaos, a cacophony grand,
For in this mad rhythm, together we stand.

Oh, the joy of the jesters that taunt us each day,
In a world full of laughs, let the nonsense hold sway.
With each twist and turn, we embrace all the wild,
In this dance of the silly, let's all be a child.

Paradoxical Paths

Two roads diverged, what a peculiar sight,
One leads to a bakery, one's dark as the night.
With croissants so flaky, it shouts, "Come and eat!"
While the shadowy path feels quite hard on the feet.

Left turns to trouble, and right goes for fun,
But what if I take both? Oh, I might weigh a ton!
I'll juggle my choices like pies in the air,
In this circus of life, we all need a pair.

The paradoxes stretch like a rubber band high,
As I flip through the choices, oh my, oh my!
I laugh through the tangle—it tickles my brain,
In this maze of delight, I feel no disdain.

So here's to the forks, and the bends in our fate,
Where chaos and laughter make life truly great.
In paths less traveled, or the ones we all know,
We'll dance through the paradox, let our humor flow.

The Algebra of Astral Adventures

In the cosmos, numbers play,
Stars calculate the night and day.
With a wink, they twist and twirl,
Math is magic, watch it swirl!

Equations dance, a cosmic jest,
Adding laughter to the quest.
Variables jump like comets bright,
In this realm of sheer delight!

Parallel lines share a secret glance,
In this universe, they prance.
They giggle in geometric glee,
Forming shapes with quirky spree!

So grab your compass, let's explore,
Algebra opens up the door.
To galaxies where jesters reign,
And numbers bring a joyful gain!

Chronicles of Celestial Confluence

In a nebula of giggling stars,
Asteroids bounce like playful cars.
Planets trade their silly hats,
While comets crisscross like acrobats!

In this confluence of cosmic cheer,
Black holes whisper, 'Come near!'
With a chuckle, they suck, then snort,
Creating chaos, a cosmic sport!

Galaxies spin in a disco dance,
Astrophysicists take a chance.
To fit that waltz within a rhyme,
While gravity plays tricks on time!

So gather 'round, let's write it down,
A chronicle of this wacky town.
Where the universe wears a smile,
And laughter stretches for many a mile!

Explorations of Existence

In the vastness, I found a cheer,
Questions bounce as if on beer.
What's the meaning, they joke and play,
Existence wears a silly bouquet!

Beams of light tease the blackened void,
While spacetime's fabric gets deployed.
The space-time continuum wears a wig,
In cosmic games, it loves to dig!

I tried to reason with the stars,
They laughed at my earthly pars.
A riddle of existence unfurled,
With nonsensical joy that swirled!

So let's embark on this grand quest,
To find the mirth within the jest.
In every twinkling, laugh we'll find,
Explorations leave no heart maligned!

Celestial Alliterations

Silly stars sprinkle silver light,
As comets careen with pure delight.
Galactic giggles grace the sky,
And planets play peek-a-boo nearby!

Dancing dust devils delight in spins,
While meteors tease with cheeky grins.
Astrophysical hilarity unfolds,
In tales of cosmic wonders told!

Fanciful flares flicker and shine,
Synchronized in patterns so fine.
Witty wishes waft through the night,
In this tapestry of joyful sight!

So let's recite this stellar song,
Where every note is whimsically strong.
Celestial alliterations in play,
Make the universe laugh and sway!

Planetary Poetics

In orbit, a cow wore a gown,
Danced circles round a sleepy town.
A comet sneezed, stars went 'Achoo!',
Why do moons have such a big view?

Jupiter's gas, a frothy delight,
Swirls of colors in the cold night.
Mars threw a party, no one was there,
Red dust flew up, in the cool evening air.

Earth rolled its eyes at the vast expanse,
Whispered to the sun, 'Don't start a dance!'
Pluto just chuckled, 'I'm still really cool,'
In this cosmic playground, we all are the fools.

The Milky Way laughs with a twinkling grin,
Galactic giggles swirling within.
Stars tell jokes beneath their bright lights,
In this whacky world of celestial sights.

Celestial Conundrums

A star tried to dress, but missed the whole point,
Its sparkly gown found itself out of joint.
Asteroids argued over their name,
'Rocky or metal? It's all just a game!'

Venus wore shades, thought she was the best,
While Mercurial minds just couldn't rest.
Neptune got dizzy from all of the spins,
Said, 'I like my mood swings; it's where my fun begins!'

Black holes debate if they're full or just shy,
Unfurling their secrets with a cosmic sigh.
Saturn played chess with rings all around,
Hoping to checkmate the lost stardust found.

The universe chuckles at space-time and beams,
While comets chase dreams and planets chase dreams.
A cosmic ballet with lots of strange moves,
In the realm of the stars, everyone grooves.

Stellar Syntax

Sentence structures in the cosmic air,
Galaxies pause, and take a fun dare.
Syntax spins like a wild shooting star,
Writing its lines from afar, oh so bizarre!

Punctuation marks hang out near the sun,
A period thought it could run just for fun!
Exclamations danced with a punchy sound,
While commas giggled on the grammar ground.

Alliteration twinkled in cosmic chime,
Words floated freely, with rhythm and rhyme.
Metaphors leaped from one star to the next,
Creating constellations, so bright and perplexed.

With every line that the stars try to craft,
The universe laughs in a sonorous draft.
Dialogue flows in the skies, oh so clever,
In this galactic tale that goes on forever.

Dimensional Dichotomies

Time hops like a bunny through alternate lanes,
Where laughter collides with the strangest of gains.
Parallel worlds with their quirky routines,
Spin yarns of cosmic riddles through unseen screens.

Dimensions giggle at their playful fate,
In twinkling spaces, they dilate and debate.
One says, 'I'm small!' the other cries, 'Gigantic!'
Together they dance in a rhythm quite frantic!

A tesseract's puzzle, both simple and grand,
Twists space and time with an elegant hand.
Infinite quirks in their playful embrace,
Like children who chase an elusive base.

As jokes slip through, the worlds intertwine,
Where absurdity finds a splendid design.
In the multiverse of giggles and glee,
Life's a funny riddle for you and for me.

Orbiting Fate

In a dance, the stars collide,
Spinning tales, they joke and bide.
Gravity pulls with a silly twist,
Even moons can't help but missed.

Roll that planet, watch it sway,
Neptune giggles, what a play!
Cosmic orbs in merry chase,
With a wink, they find their place.

Dimensions of Delight

Warp the space and time we know,
In silliness, the laughter flows.
Parallel worlds, oh what a mess,
Tangled socks in cosmic dress.

Jump through dimensions, take a peek,
Oddities make laughter peak.
Twisting paths where humor grows,
In every bend, a giggle shows.

Quantum Whispers

In tiny realms where quirks reside,
Particles play, they giggle wide.
Heisenberg's fun with jokes unspun,
Uncertainty brings laughs to run.

Superposition's playful game,
Cats in boxes, none are the same.
What's real? The fun's a muddled mix,
Quantum quirks, the best of tricks.

Celestial Synchronicity

Stars aligned in cosmic jest,
Synchronizing in their quest.
Planets twirling, laughing round,
In this ballet, joy is found.

Comets zoom with a wink and grin,
Chasing laughter, let's begin.
Galaxies swirl, in sync they flow,
A cosmic giggle, a stellar show.

Celestial Echoes

In the sky, the stars do wink,
A cosmic joke, what do you think?
Galaxies dance, a silly prance,
While comets giggle in a trance.

The moon wears socks upon its feet,
Jupiter bounces to a groovy beat.
Saturn spins, its rings a swirl,
As funny clouds begin to twirl.

Space-time bends like a rubber band,
Aliens play with a wobbly hand.
Laughter echoes through the night,
In a universe that's pure delight.

So heed the stars, don't miss the fun,
In this galactic dance, we all will run.
With each tick-tock and cosmic cheer,
The universe smiles, drawing near.

The Music of the Spheres

The planets sing in perfect tune,
Strumming stars beneath the moon.
A symphony of cosmic range,
With aliens playing a hearty exchange.

Venus hums a silly song,
While Earth just dances all night long.
Mars plays drums made of red dust,
A playful beat that's hard to trust.

From the sun, we hear a glare,
As laughter floats upon the air.
Each orbit's note, a joyful sound,
In this strange band, we're all around.

So let us join this merry choir,
With stars and moons our hearts desire.
In the music that never fades,
Life's a cosmic parade!

Temporal Tides

Time flows like jelly on a plate,
With otters surfing, it's first-rate.
Past and future twist and twirl,
As seconds giggle and whirl.

A clock that clucks and crows at dawn,
As minutes trot off, and then they're gone.
Oh, look! A second flies a kite,
While hours race with all their might.

Waves of laughter wash the shore,
Each tick a giggle, who could ask for more?
Time takes breaks for a cosmic sip,
In between each tick and trip.

So let us play with these temporal tides,
With laughter dancing as our guide.
In this ocean, we can glide,
Where time itself is full of pride.

Cosmic Kaleidoscope

Through a scope, the colors burst,
A swirling view, it's quite the first.
With every twist, the hues collide,
In this funny place, you'll want to glide.

Stars are marbles in a box,
Rolling 'round like playful ox.
Nebulas paint with silly flair,
While cosmic critters dance in air.

Galaxies wobble in delight,
Spinning tales through the starry night.
A humorous play, a joyful scope,
In this universe of endless hope.

So peek inside, there's much to see,
Imagination runs wild and free.
In this kaleidoscope of bliss,
You'll find the laughter you can't miss.

The Fabric of Forever

In threads of fate, we weave and spin,
A sock for a shoe that may never grin.
Dancing with time in a comical race,
Wearing mismatched shoes, a peculiar grace.

The clocks all giggle, they lose their tick,
A turtle named Barry runs marathons quick.
We trip over laughter, a bright yellow shoelace,
In this crazy quilt of an oddball space.

Space Between Stars

Between each twinkle, a joke takes flight,
A cow jumps high, it's a truly odd sight.
Planets play tag in a solar game,
While asteroids chuckle, none feel the shame.

A comet zooms by with a vibrant tail,
It whispers sweet nothings, a starry ale.
While meteors tumble, they fall with a shout,
"Catch us, if you can, or just take us out!"

Universal Journeys

A spaceship painted in polka-dot glee,
Steering through space, sipping cosmic tea.
Aliens giggle with three wiggly arms,
Trading their snacks for earthling charms.

Mars hosts a party with little green friends,
They dance like worms 'til the daylight ends.
Galaxies swirl in a dizzying spin,
Who knew so much fun could be found within?

The Harmony of Happenstance

In the universe's joke, we all play a part,
A giraffe in a boat with a lollipop heart.
Planets collide with a comedic clash,
Turning black holes into a cosmic smash.

Chance encounters lead to laughter so bright,
Like fireflies cracking jokes in the night.
So let's toast to the whimsy, the odd, and the free,
In this quicksilver dance, just you wait and see!

The Lexicon of Light

In a world where photons dance,
Words take flight, they spin and prance.
A quark's a joke, a neutron's glee,
In this bright lexicon, you'll see.

Giggles echo, atoms sing,
This is the fun that science brings.
Light years may stretch, but time plays tricks,
A paradox wrapped in clever quips.

So zoom with me through endless space,
Where every particle finds its place.
Quantum leaps and starlit sights,
Let's chuckle through these cosmic nights.

In laughter's glow, we find our way,
Through dark matter, we'll whimsically sway.
So grab your pens, let's make it bright,
In this lexicon of sheer delight.

Comets and Continuums

A comet zips, a streak of fun,
It winks at time, it's on the run.
Continuums bend, but who cares?
We're catching laughs in cosmic snares.

Jokes collide in stellar flight,
Gravity's pull can't dim our light.
Black holes laugh, they suck things in,
But with a grin, we'll twirl and spin.

Einstein chuckles in the night sky,
As laughter lands like confetti high.
Each paradox a playful clue,
In this vast dance, it's me and you.

So let's embrace this starry spree,
With comets, quips, and glee, you see.
Continuums twirl in joyful mirth,
As we explode with giggles, embracing earth.

Eternal Embers

From the ashes, laughter glows,
Eternal embers, how it shows!
Physics chuckles, ignites the night,
Each spark of joy, a pure delight.

Time's a jester, tricks we play,
Poking fun in a silly way.
With every tick, a giggle bursts,
In this timeline, try not to thirst.

Stars wink down with playful glee,
As comets dance with jests, you see.
Supernovas explode in rhyme,
Creating space for laughing time.

So let's ignite these cosmic fires,
With jokes and joy, fulfill our desires.
Eternal embers of mirth abound,
In this universe, joy is found.

Fractals of Fate

Fractals twirling in a dizzy haze,
Life's puzzles stretch in merry ways.
Infinity giggles with every turn,
In patterns where our passions burn.

Quantum quirks and silly fate,
Round and round, we contemplate.
Reality bends in fractal charm,
Wrapped in humor, oh, what a balm!

Tickle your mind with fractal fun,
As chances weave, we've just begun.
The universe laughs, oh how it glows,
In this tapestry, laughter flows.

So join the dance of fate's delight,
In fractals we find our playful flight.
With every twist and silly state,
We'll savor the fun in this wild fate.

Cosmic Conversations

In a galaxy far and wide,
Stars twinkle while comets glide.
Aliens laugh and play peek,
Communicating in a cosmic squeak.

Planets teeter on their own spins,
Bouncing in orbit, it's where fun begins.
Jupiter jests, with a belt so grand,
While Saturn plays in a ringed band.

Black holes yawn, they take in the light,
Sucking up jokes, oh what a sight!
While meteors scribble their funny lines,
Across the sky, like playful signs.

Galactic games, with no one to see,
Stars trade stories over cosmic tea.
With laughter echoing through the vast night,
It's a universe where joy takes flight.

Gravity's Gait

Gravity's got a clumsy walk,
Trips over clouds while others gawk.
It pulls us in with such a dance,
Falling for earth at every chance.

Planets wobble in their parade,
Falling down with a playful cascade.
Stars giggle as they crush,
While moons twirl in a gentle hush.

If gravity could wear some shoes,
They'd be oversized, with silly hues.
Each step a stumble, a playful roll,
Keeping planets in a funny patrol.

So when you trip, don't take the blame,
It's just gravity playing its silly game.
In this dance of worlds both big and small,
Laughter might just lift us all.

Echoes of Existence

In the silence of space, echoes play,
Whispers of stars in a funny ballet.
Nebulas giggle with colors so bright,
Painting the cosmos in joyful light.

Time has a way of skipping about,
Telling silly tales that make us shout.
With each tick-tock, a chuckle unfolds,
As the universe shares its stories bold.

If shadows could speak, they'd tell you this,
Every fleeting moment has a cosmic twist.
From black hole jokes to light-year fables,
Existence is rich, as laughter enables.

So laugh with the stars, let the echoes rouse,
The funny side of life that everyone vows.
In every particle, joy's little grace,
Echoes of existence fill all of space.

Timeless Tales

Once upon a time, in a cosmic nook,
Where black holes were chefs, and stars wrote the book.
Gravity's a prankster, or so they say,
Pulling everyone in, to join the play.

Comets raced with tales to tell,
Of interstellar love and how they fell.
Stardust sprinkled with jokes on the side,
Making the Milky Way giggle with pride.

In the timeless realm where light bends slow,
Time travelers stumble, putting on a show.
Each time they slip, laughter fills the air,
As the universe bask in its funny flair.

So gather around for a joke or two,
In this timeless tale, there's room for you.
In a world where the absurd is the norm,
Let's dance in the cosmos, where laughter is warm.

A Symphony of Stars

In the night, the stars do dance,
Winking lights in cosmic pants.
They giggle, twirl, and puff out beams,
Making wishes, chasing dreams.

Through the void, they sing a tune,
Of jellybeans and silly moons.
With every flicker, they declare,
'Life's just better up in the air!'

So grab a snack and take a seat,
Join the stars for a cosmic treat.
For in this symphony it's clear,
Laughter echoes far and near.

Cosmic Currents

Floating through the galaxy's snack,
Riding waves upon a cosmic track.
Stars surf on beams of light so bright,
Sipping stardust with delight.

Comets dash in flashy styles,
Spinning tales, sharing smiles.
Galactic gags and playful flair,
They chase each other through the air.

Planets giggle, moons throw pies,
As meteors wink and shoot through skies.
In this dance of grand design,
Laughter's found where stars align.

Tapestry of Time

In the weave of space and time,
Threads of joy in perfect rhyme.
Knots of laughter, twists of fate,
Stitching fun – it's never late.

Tick-tock to the cosmic beat,
Making mischief, oh so sweet.
Yesterday's yarn, tomorrow's cheer,
Stitching memories far and near.

With each loop, a tale that's spun,
Of silly antics, endless fun.
This tapestry so grand and wide,
Pulls you in for a laughter ride.

Nebulae Narratives

In a cloud of colors, vibrant and bold,
Nebulae whisper stories untold.
They giggle between the stars so bright,
Spinning tales of cosmic flight.

With puffs of pink and shades of blue,
Each one claims a joke or two.
'Why did the star leap and shine?
To outglow the sun! It's just divine!'

They drape the sky in laughter's art,
Where starlight weaves a cosmic heart.
So join the fun in this astral spree,
With nebulae tales, it's pure glee!

Unraveling the Threads of Infinity

In the fabric of time, we spin and weave,
A sock in one hand, a lifetime to believe.
Count the stitches, can't go wrong,
Yet it always ends up like a twisted song.

Cosmic yarn balls, they tangle and roll,
Each loop a giggle, each knot a goal.
When we try to knit in a steady line,
A cosmic hiccup makes it all align.

Space-time's a joke, can't you see?
Why did the photon need a key?
To open the door to a parallel sphere,
Where laughter and logic don't always adhere.

So let's twist and turn through this grand design,
In the game of the universe, forever we dine.
With jokes that expand like the stars in the night,
We'll dance with delight, turning dark into light.

Starlit Paradox in Twilight's Embrace

As the sun dips low, the stars come to play,
They wink with ideas that frolic and sway.
A paradox lives in the twilight's soft glow,
Laughing at logic, putting on quite a show.

Why does the moon insist on being round?
While gravity keeps all its friends on the ground?
In the dance of the night, they swing and they sway,
A cosmic carnival, come join the ballet!

A comet or two on the Ferris wheel spin,
Each loop and each twirl, let the laughter begin.
What's dark matter? Just a joke that we tell,
Sitting around like a celestial shell.

So under the stars, let's giggle and scheme,
With paradoxical thoughts, we'll float and we'll beam.
Like shadows that trace where the starlight will roam,
We'll wrap up the night, calling the cosmos home.

Echoes of the Universal Song

In the symphony grand, where the galaxies hum,
Each note is an echo, a riddle, a drum.
Plucking the strings of reality's tune,
The universe winks, like a mischievous moon.

Time trips on itself, what a clumsy old chap,
With beats that are random, it's hard not to clap.
When quarks and leptons decide to engage,
They jazz up the night from the cosmic-stage.

In the hall of the stars, the melodies play,
Creating a chorus, both weird and cliche.
What's that we hear? A black hole's old joke,
It swallows the punchline; laughter's bespoke!

So let's harmonize joy from each star to each moon,
With echoes that linger, let's dance to the tune.
For in every dimension, we'll sing and we'll soar,
In this universal melody, forevermore.

Where Moments Collide and Swirl

Where seconds collide, like bugs on a screen,
Time giggles and spins, a chaotic machine.
A tick that ponders, a tock out of phase,
Creating a ruckus in time's funny maze.

Past and present get tangled in thread,
A clock's old story seems silly instead.
In the whirl of the now, as futures take flight,
We chuckle at the sight of a paradox bright.

So grab your time coat, let's jump and let's hop,
Through moments that flop, where hiccups don't stop.
What if you're late? Just a twist in the play,
Where time doesn't judge; it just giggles away!

With laughter in loops, and memories thrown,
Let's toast to the moments we've joyfully blown.
In the whirl of our days, we embrace every swirl,
Together, we dance in this time-twisted whirl.

The Dance of Destinies

In a universe wide, we waltz with fate,
Skipping on stardust, we laugh, don't wait.
Comets do cha-chas, planets in spin,
Even the sun grins, let the dance begin!

Twinkling our toes on the Milky Way's bridge,
Gravity drops us, but oh, what a ridge!
Stars play the fiddle, moons keep the beat,
In this cosmic party, we just can't retreat!

Galaxies swirl like partners in grace,
In the vastness of space, we find our place.
We all trip and tumble, it's all just for fun,
In the dance of the cosmos, we're never outdone!

So here's to the jig of the bright and the bold,
With each step we take, new destinies unfold.
We'll shuffle and slide till there's no more to see,
In the dance of the ages, come shake it with me!

Celestial Codas

In the sky's grand theater, stars sing their parts,
With rhythms of laughter, they warm up our hearts.
Nebulae hum tunes, like jazz in the night,
While black holes can't dance, but they swallow the light!

Planets play maracas, asteroids clap hands,
We ride cosmic rhythms through faraway lands.
The sun shines a spotlight; it's showtime, you see,
A cosmic cabaret, come laugh along with me!

Galactic unicorns prance, they twirl with delight,
As meteors zoom past, putting on quite a fright.
The universe giggles at everything near,
In celestial codas, there's always good cheer!

So take up your seat in this stellar parade,
With laughter and joy, let no moment fade.
Cosmic ballads resound in this grand jubilee,
Join the funny saga we're all meant to be!

Black Hole Ballads

In the dark of a black hole, there's music untold,
With a twist of wild notes, like a tale of old.
Gravity's tug pulls at your shoelace tight,
But oh, what a melody, the stars shine bright!

With a spin and a twirl, we sing with a grin,
As matter gets lost, we let the fun in.
Singing sweet ballads of what once was there,
We giggle and tease, not a worry or care!

Space-time starts dancing, it sways to our song,
Even the comets join in the throng.
Whispering secrets of worlds that we've missed,
While we're swirling in black holes, in cosmic bliss!

So if you get swallowed by gravity's cheer,
Remember the laughter that brought you right here.
In the depths of creation, let joy take the lead,
With black hole ballads, we're all truly freed!

Cosmic Cartwheels

With a flip and a roll, we launch into space,
Cosmic cartwheels whirling, they set the pace.
Nebulas giggle as galaxies spin,
While quarks do the twist; it's a win-win win!

Stardust thrown wide on this celestial ground,
As comets do tumbles, oh, isn't it sound?
Planets take flight, off to the side,
With their moon buddies cheering, it's quite the ride!

So come join the fun, grab your cosmic pair,
In the dance of the stars, we take to the air.
With laughter and whimsy, we dive and we swirl,
In cosmic cartwheels, let your laughter unfurl!

For in the large tapestry of the night sky,
Each spin brings us closer, oh my, oh my!
In this quirky ballet, we'll twirl till we gleam,
Cosmic cartwheels unite us, like a dream within a dream!

Space-Time Serenade in the Dark

In a galaxy far, far away,
Where socks and spoons often play,
The clock spins in a wobbly way,
   Making even Einstein sway.

Stars dance like they're in a trance,
While comets try their luck at a chance,
A black hole sings a tune so dense,
   Even planets join in the prance.

Cosmic hiccups fill the night,
As meteors compete in a meteor fight,
Gravity laughs, causing delight,
While aliens make shadow puppets in flight.

So grab your telescope, don't be late,
Join the space jam, it's really great,
   In the dark, let's celebrate,
The quirks that make the cosmos rotate.

Dimensions of Love Beyond Time

In a realm where love wears a hat,
And time gets lost chasing a cat,
Hearts tick tock like an old phat rat,
While seconds flirt with acrobatic chat.

Parallel lovers wink from afar,
In multiple worlds where dreams are bizarre,
Each kiss a step towards the bizarre,
While hugs are measured by a cosmic jar.

A heartbeat echoes, a spectral tune,
As starlight dances with the moon,
They break the rules, it's quite a boon,
Sipping joy in a silver cocoon.

Through time and space, they zoom, they jest,
In dimensions where love is a quest,
No boundaries here, just be your best,
In this timeless, wacky love fest.

Fractals of Existence and Light

In patterns so curious, round and round,
Even the light beams get unwound,
Spirals of giggles swirl all around,
Where logic takes a break and confounds.

Each twist a tumble, a cosmic dance,
Reflections of joy in a child's glance,
A fractal of laughter, a merry chance,
As shadows and echoes join in the prance.

Colors collide, a vibrant riot,
While photons party, oh what a diet,
If fun was a force, this would be the quiet,
In each little flicker, we can't help but try it.

So spin with me through the fractal haze,
Where reason gives way to delightful craze,
In this kaleidoscope of funny ways,
Life's a playful puzzle, let's stack the rays.

A Journey Through the Cosmic Maze

In a maze made of stars and whimsy,
Where laughter echoes, never flimsy,
Einstein's theories seem quite flimsy,
As we navigate with a cosmic flimsy.

Each turn reveals a new surprise,
Like finding candy in moonlit skies,
With every twist, our spirits rise,
In this cosmic game where nonsense flies.

Black holes giggle as we slip and slide,
Through wormholes, we take our joyride,
Planets cheer, in colors wide,
In this maze where wonders abide.

So take my hand, let's lose our way,
In this playful universe on display,
Through twists and turns, forever sway,
In laughter's embrace, we'll boldly play.

www.ingramcontent.com/pod-product-compliance
Lightning Source LLC
Chambersburg PA
CBHW051700160426
43209CB00004B/967